W9-CHT-736

What people say about Golf & the Art of Customer Service

"The hands down best book I've ever read on customer service. Your book has the power to transform an organization to become truly customer centric. It is the *Who Moved my Cheese* of customer service."
- **Janine Regosin, Director Community Relations, Senior Bridge**

"This seemingly simple and warm story is bigger than the sum of its parts. Fundamental truths come to life and it shows how we all become stronger and happier by serving others. Highly recommended."
- **Gary Glynn, President, U.S. Steel and Carnegie Pension Fund**

"Working with celebrities I understand the importance of exceptional customer service, and this book provides the insights into creating that unique customer experience."
- **Tisha Fein, Co-Producer, The Grammy Awards**

"Any sales or customer service team incorporating the U Factor will significantly increase client loyalty. A must read for every salesperson."
- **Bruce F. Reynolds, Vice President Sales, Chicken of the Sea International**

"I was surprised how quickly I was hooked. It's all you need to know in a nutshell. An art piece. Anyone who runs a service business must read this and then give a copy to each employee when they go through orientation."
- **Kay Ullman, Office Coordinator, Carlson Physical Therapy**

"I would certainly give my business to any organization that learns the lessons of your gem of a book."
- Joanna Schaffer, Assistant Vice President, Marsh USA Inc.

"You provide the recipe for any organization to significantly increase their sales through service. What I love about your book is that it's fast, it's focused, it's powerful."
- Michael J. Mulligan, CEO Advanced Business Group, Inc.

"A really great short read that summarizes the key principles of customer service in the healthcare environment."
- Dr. Robert Carroll, Emergency Department Chairman, Eastern Ct. Health Network, Inc.

"This unique book provides hands on tools to increase an organization's effectiveness in business."
- William M. Mooney, Jr., President, The Westchester County Association

"The concepts are so easy to understand and so easy to communicate to others."
- Marianne Muise, Principal, Healthcare Management Solutions LLC

"This is a simple yet profound book."
- Martha Troup, Manager, International Rock Band INXS with over 30 million records sold

"This book is a must read for all healthcare professionals."
- Dr. Jeffrey Borenstein, CEO, The Holliswood Hospital, Host Healthy Minds TV show

GOLF & THE ART OF

CUSTOMER SERVICE

The Reiss Brothers

BEAR Reissource Books

GOLF & THE ART OF CUSTOMER SERVICE

Library of Congress Control Number: 2006922704

ISBN 0-9779001-9-3

WHY WE WROTE THIS BOOK

Customer service means business. A recent J.D. Powers five-year study revealed that organizations which improved customer service increased shareholder value by 52%, while those organizations whose service declined lost 28% of their value. If you want to improve your organization's performance, you must start with the customer experience.

Too often customer service is viewed as an afterthought, when it should actually drive your brand. The question is how to get all of your employees on the same page so that you can truly become customer centric. This book may well be the first book in America to share customer service from the "inside out" -- in an easy to read story that everyone can relate to. Embedded in the story are 27 customer service tools that can jumpstart the process of change.

It is our hope that this book will enable everyone, from CEO to front line staff, to work together to enhance the customer experience and transform their organization.

Business starts with your customer.

Being a new golfer, I have been amazed by the deep lessons that golf has to teach us about business and life.

I dedicate this book to the love of my life – my wife Barbara, and to my three greatest inspirations: James, Josh and Molly.
- Robert Reiss

As a writer I am thankful for all that I have learned throughout this book's journey. As a performer I am grateful for the gift to share with a new audience.
- Michael Reiss

Foreword

Having worked 27 years in the hospital business, the last 8 as Griffin Hospital's CEO, I recognize the importance of building a patient centered culture where employees are fulfilled by and passionate about their work.

I was excited to discover *Golf & the Art of Customer Service*. The content and insights in this book are uncanny. The Reiss brothers distill complex concepts and make them easy to understand in a compelling way. This book should resonate with staff; it is a great way to start a dialogue within an organization that can lead to focus, alignment and a more customer centric culture.

The service expectation of hospital patients is generally higher than that of customers in other industries, as it is often more than just the patient's money that is on the line. *Golf & the Art of Customer Service* provides the right tools to build employee pride and deliver exemplary hospital customer service. And I believe that if you can satisfy demanding hospital customers, you can produce customer satisfaction anywhere.

- Patrick Charmel, President & CEO Griffin Health Services Corporation -- *Fortune Magazine's* **top five Best Companies to Work For in America 2006 -- Co-Author Putting Patients First, Jossey-Bass 2003**

Contents

Acknowledgements

We would like to thank those who have brought wisdom, insights and energy to this book:

Peter Belmont, Michele Bibb, Jubily Boy, Patrick Charmel, Bonnie Depp, Ruth Ford, Richard Goldberg, Robert Greenfield, Patti Hammond, Julie Jansen, Ben Kaplan, Paul Leslie, Harriet Levine, Stuart R. Levine, Deidre McClain, Mary Mong, Donna Moore, Michael Mulligan, John Papa, Janine Regosin, Alvin H. Reiss, Ellen Reiss, Steven Reiss, Walter Timoshenko, Martha Troup, Kay Ullman, Scott Ventrella, Mark Vickery, Art Weintraub, and Nancy Zelenock.

In memory of the inspiration of "Trombone" Sam.

And a special thanks to the creative genius and heart of Ellen Looyen.

Passing the Torch

It all began with Goldie. After visiting a dying patient at a hospital in Brooklyn New York, she wondered why this patient couldn't have more comfort and dignity. Goldie began the arduous fundraising task, which resulted in the opening of what many consider the first "hospice" in America. The Home for the Incurables opened on April 24, 1929.

Her daughter Anne built on this legacy and spent much of her life comforting and entertaining hospital patients.

Perhaps this is why I, Anne's son, went into the non-profit field as a writer and teacher.

And now it has come full circle. I am proud of Robert and Michael. They are my sons.

- Alvin H. Reiss

Prologue

I find that effective customer service at its essence rests squarely upon a foundation of accessibility, perceived respect, and responsiveness. We, as a society, maintain an inherent need to be heard and to have our concerns validated. All too often, cursory, abrupt and dismissive responses by ill-trained front-line personnel routinely escalate matters that may otherwise find swift resolution and, more importantly, maintain the valued customer-business relationship.

While "canned" or scripted responses may serve a purpose, they often fall short of effective responsiveness and – when handled poorly – imbue in the customer a sense of insignificance. While the customer service representative may have dealt with hundreds of customer problems that same day, the well-trained staffer with the correct tools will embrace each customer problem as though it were their first priority.

If handled correctly, even a customer who fails to receive all that they are seeking may still be left with a cathartic sense of closure; they have been taken seriously and treated with the respect that they expect and deserve.

The cost-benefit analysis of customer service is self-evident. Spending the time, effort and resources for effective, consistent and responsive service should be a priority for any business. In my personal opinion, Golf & the Art of Customer Service provides the tools and captures a message that the American business community needs to remember – quality customer service is simply smart business.

-Brian Rauer, Executive Director, The Better Business Bureau, Mid-Hudson, NY & General Counsel, The Better Business Bureau serving Metro NY, Inc.
*The views expressed herein are the personal opinion of the writer and do not necessarily represent the views of the organization with which he is affiliated.

PART ONE

Last Shot

Jack looked at the fairway. He knew if he hit the shot he'd win the game. If not he would lose.

It was Saturday morning and Jack was playing golf with his best friend Ted at the public golf course.

Jack had started playing golf five years earlier and had really fallen in love with the game. Before he ever played he was a bit intimidated. He thought it would be too expensive, too difficult, and take too long. He thought he'd have to join some exclusive club just to play a game he'd be lousy at. Then a co-worker, after a particularly rough day on the job, said he'd take Jack to a golf driving range where they could "blow off some steam."

It was a revelation. For a few dollars Jack had a bucket of balls and a club and could hit away for half an hour. As lousy as he hit the ball it was so much fun, and some of his shots actually went flying straight.

For the cost of lunch Jack would play nine holes in two hours and completely unwind. Like so many people he couldn't get enough and was always looking to improve his game.

Again Jack looked at his golf ball resting on the tee. Golf was a game of concentration. Up until the eighth hole Jack's concentration had been up to par. But now as he prepared for his final drive, his concentration began to slip away.

Truth was Jack and Ted's golf outing had been

scheduled for the following Saturday, but Jack asked if they could move it up a week. Golf usually cleared Jack's head and relaxed him.

Four days earlier a mysterious e-mail had appeared on Jack's desk. All it said was "prepare for change." Not the most comforting e-mail with the rumors spreading throughout the hospital about potential layoffs. Then later that afternoon Jack received a call from the hospital president to meet in her office the following Monday morning.

Jack had been at the hospital for eight years, the last five in the accounting department. Although he started as an administrative assistant/word processor, Jack had worked hard and steadily moved up the ladder in responsibility and salary. Jack believed if he stayed on path he'd be able to buy a house in a few years. But now he questioned that assumption.

"Excuse me, Ted. Let me just take a second to regain my bearings."

"Sure thing, Jack. I did the math in my head too, and I know a good drive will seal the deal," Ted said with a smile and a chuckle. Although they were the best of friends, when it came to golf, they were fiercely competitive.

Jack walked a good twenty feet away from the tee letting Ted know he needed a few moments to regroup. As Jack took in a few deep breaths of open air and the fresh smell of cut grass he heard Ted call out to someone.

"Hi, Peter."

"Hello, Ted, how are you?" Jack heard a deep, relaxed

voice resonate from 25 feet away.

"Good, Peter, just trying to stay on my game," Ted answered in a voice more serious than his usually light-hearted self.

"Just remember, the show's right here," the deep voice bellowed back.

The show's right here. What does that mean, Jack thought.

"A friend of yours?" Jack asked, as he glanced back to get a glimpse of the man attached to the voice.

"Actually he's a golf pro. Played in some tournaments back in the day. Was even once named the most complete golf teacher." Ted said in a tone that asked for a certain level of reverence.

"Really?" As Jack replied, he turned around to see a stately man with broad shoulders and a thick silver mane of hair, in his mid-seventies, walking toward the clubhouse. The man strode away with a relaxed confidence that reminded Jack of an actor from another era.

"What does he mean by the show's right here?" Jack asked. His curiosity about this man was now piqued.

"It's kind of hard to explain, but it sort of means that the show's right there," Ted replied, pointing to Jack's golf ball resting on the tee.

Jack looked down at his golf ball, confused. He then took a deep breath, drew back his club, and took a hard swing. The ball went directly into the trees. Some show, Jack thought.

All Fired Up

Eight hard years of work had come to this, Jack thought, as he walked down the corridor of the fourth floor to the elevator. He feared he was about to be fired.

Everyone knew the hospital wasn't in great shape and layoffs hung over their heads like dark rain clouds. They were all just counting the minutes to the thunder and lightning, and Jack thought his minute might be up.

As he passed the nurses and other employees on the first floor he saw it on their faces. Everyone had that deer-in-the-headlights look. Nurses were afraid to really talk with patients for fear that something could be misunderstood and they could be sued or lose their license. Employees were scared to talk to their managers out of fear of being fired. An entire institution was running scared. Everyone was afraid of what might happen next yet it looked like it was Jack's head that was about to go on the chopping block.

What would Jack tell his wife? That the past few years while he buried himself in work not spending enough quality time with her and their daughter Alex had been in vain?

As Jack entered Bochard's outer office her secretary smiled. "She's expecting you."

Jack took a deep measured breath and walked into Bochard's office prepared to meet his fate.

Jack looked at Bochard sitting in her large red leather chair. Bochard had the regal look you might see in a painting hanging over the fireplace of a stately mansion.

Many employees at the hospital found her more than a bit intimidating.

"Please, Jack, have a seat," Bochard said as she motioned to the black straight-back chair in front of her desk. Jack nodded and sat down.

"So, I must say, Jack, I was impressed with the way you worked with some of our customers in that situation last quarter with billing."

"Thank you," Jack politely nodded.

"You're not only good with numbers, but you seem to have a sense of how to handle people."

"Thank you, Ms. Bochard."

"Which brings me to the reason I brought you here today. I don't think accounting is the best fit for you."

Could the compliments be a setup, Jack thought? Was he one moment away from being fired? He looked Bochard directly in the eyes ready to hear whatever she had to say.

One Flight Down

"Make a wish, Jack," Janice encouraged enthusiastically. As Jack blew out the candles for his going-away party he tried to put on a sad face, one that said how much he'd miss everyone in the accounting department. The truth was that Jack was only moving one flight down, had actually received a small raise from Bochard, and was happy to be the new manager of the customer service department.

That afternoon Bochard had explained why she gave Jack the job. She thought his finance background might help provide a practical perspective on customer service. Basically, Bochard expected Jack to reduce the customer complaint response time and find a way to resolve complaints more efficiently.

To be honest, Jack was also happy to be leaving an environment where all conversation revolved around who might lose their jobs, and when. That was the one thing about accounting; you saw the numbers, and they weren't always pretty. Plus, Jack reasoned customer service was a small department, and a less likely target for layoffs.

"I'm going to miss you all so much, especially Janice's herbal tea," Jack said. Everyone laughed. "It seems like only yesterday we were newly hired, and running around like chickens with their heads cut off."

"Jack, where you're going, you won't need a head." Leave it to Neil to throw a little sarcasm into the soup. There was an uncomfortable pause in the festivities of the room, until Jack smiled and gave a little laugh, and everyone else joined in. Neil could have that effect on people. At first Jack thought Neil was genuinely a mean-spirited person, but through time Jack realized Neil was just so terrified of losing his job that he would do anything to protect it.

Jack knew the accounting department resented the customer service department. Customer service was considered a fluff department. No numbers, no deadlines. Just smile and play nice. What they were all thinking, but not saying–everyone except for Neil–was that Jack was going to easy street.

The reality was that since the threat of layoffs all departments thought of themselves as alone and for themselves. It was like they were all contestants on "The Apprentice," just praying not to hear those fateful words, "You're fired."

"Maybe I'll sneak up for a cup," Jack said, smiling at Janice.

Again the warmth returned to the room. Then the phone rang. The call was from the nursing staff. Apparently there was a lot of noise was coming from an elderly patient suffering from leukemia, in the 4D unit. The man, Bernie Seethers, was yelling that it took too long for the nurses to respond when he rang the call bell. Although Jack was still celebrating his promotion, and had not officially taken the leadership role in the customer service department, he immediately headed down to 4D.

"A damn two hours I tell you!" Jack heard the elderly man shouting at two nurses.

"Mr. Seethers, I think you might be exaggerating just a bit. Once again we're sorry for the delay, but you're not the only patient at this hospital, and we can't just cater instantly to your individual needs." A nurse spoke sternly to the cantankerous old man.

Maybe, Jack thought, this is what customer service was really about.

An Eve-ning Out

Jack had made reservations for Angelino's Restaurant, and the sitter was coming at seven thirty. Jack was looking forward to celebrating with his wife Eve.

Jack appreciated that Eve was always there to support

him. He also knew that she was wiser than she often let on. As the waiter showed them to their table, Jack was thinking that maybe his new job would help him and Eve regain the closeness they once shared. Jack knew the past few years of job-related stress had definitely drained some of the magic out of their relationship. Now he might finally have money to buy her something special, maybe even go on a long-overdo vacation.

"So how was the party?" Eve asked with a smile.

"It was nice, but I was really thinking about tonight. It's been a long time since we've gone out," Jack said in his warmest voice.

"I know. Do you remember the last time we were here?" Eve asked, as she looked at Jack again with an inquisitive smile.

"I do. Your parents sent us here for our anniversary while they watched Alex."

Eve looked impressed. "So did Bochard show up at the party?"

"No, but I didn't think she would. It's not her style. You know she's that no-tears, captain of industry type. Plus, I think she knows what the accounting department thinks of the customer service department."

"Was that ever brought up?" Eve asked.

"No, other than the usual dark sarcasm from Neil, it was like I was just going away somewhere, rather than one floor down to customer service."

"Neil's jealous of you, honey. He wishes he was the one

getting the promotion. Something about him really concerns me."

"Oh, he's all right. He's just scared of losing his own job," Jack said, trying to ease a worry he heard in Eve's voice.

"Please, just try to keep your distance from him."

"I'll be fine. Really."

"Just try."

"I promise," Jack said, smiling. "And I also promise to spend more quality time with you and Alex. Things are going to change," Jack warmly added as he looked into Eve's eyes.

Eight years ago, when Jack and Eve married, everything seemed perfect, but work had really put a strain on their relationship. They didn't talk or communicate like they used to. They used to look at one another and, without saying a word, each would know what the other was thinking. Now they didn't have a clue. Things had changed. Eve was patient, but Jack sensed that deep down she wasn't really happy. Somehow Eve had found a way to balance her substitute teaching job and a home life, but it was more difficult for Jack. He knew he had to find a way to get the closeness back, and thought maybe this new job with some more money and free time might help.

Taking Care of Business

Jack's staff consisted of six people. Timothy, whom he had heard really good things about, handled customer complaints. Everyone introduced themselves, and seemed pleasant enough. Maybe customer service would be an easy fit.

As Jack settled at his desk, Timothy explained how the complaints were filed, and about the weekly report that was sent to Bochard's office.

"So Bochard receives a report every week?" Jack asked.

"Like clockwork," Timothy said. "You know Bouchard fired Ben Johnson, the last head of customer service, because of the increase in customer complaint response time over the last year. Now I don't think it was all Johnson's fault, there's really a lot to stay on top of."

"I can imagine," Jack said while nodding his head and digesting this new information.

"I've seen some corporate e-mails pass my desk and I know that Bochard is under serious pressure from the board. She's a strong executive but even at her position, I think she's just overworked. I think the board saw a potential financial upturn from improving customer service and creating more referrals. Which I imagine is why she chose someone on the inside. Someone who maybe could see the real inner workings. That would be you."

Timothy then pulled Jack aside, so the other people in the office couldn't hear, and whispered, "This one just came across my desk. It's an e-mail from Neil in accounting, to Bochard, saying the customer service department is the least efficient department in the hospital." Timothy, with a nervous look on his face, handed Jack the e-mail.

"Thanks, Timothy."

"Should we be worried?"

"Business as usual. Don't give it a second thought," Jack said to Timothy with a reassuring smile.

Truth was, Jack was a little annoyed that Neil's negative aura was headed toward customer service, and he didn't want Timothy or anyone else to be impacted.

Could Bochard have put Jack in a situation where she thought he'd fail, and then have just cause for his dismissal? After all, what did he really know about customer service?

Help Wanted

Golf always seemed to help Jack get on track with all aspects of his life, so he decided to book a golf lesson for the following Saturday with the mysterious golf pro he had seen on the course that day with Ted.

Saturday was gray and overcast. As Jack waited by the driving range he saw the graceful older man stride over to him with the ease of someone who was never in a rush yet always on time. Peter greeted Jack with a broad smile and a firm handshake.

"So are you ready to learn to let the game of golf work for you?" Peter asked with a soft tone and a serious look.

"Well, I'm ready to try," Jack answered, knowing that he had been a reasonable athlete in his day and never shied away from competition.

"Golf really boils down to three main types of shots," Peter explained. "First the drive, which gets the ball down the fairway; second, the approach shot to reach the green;

third, the putt, where you tap the ball in the hole. And that's it." Peter smiled. That made it seem much easier than Jack knew it would actually be.

"Today we're going to attack your drive, so we can do the whole lesson on the driving range. Next time we'll get on the course," Peter said.

"Sounds good," Jack politely answered.

"So let's see your swing," Peter said with a relaxed grin.

Jack tried to remember everything he had learned about golf in the past. How were his feet, his hips, his shoulders, his elbows, his grip?

"Just relax and swing," Peter assured Jack in his deep, soothing voice.

Jack hit a decent shot–about 200 yards, and it didn't slice.

"Not bad. Let's see it again."

I'm back, Jack thought, and then sliced the ball 150 yards into the trees.

"OK, now tell me what you're thinking about as you drive," Peter asked.

"Well, I'm thinking about all of the different parts. How wide are my feet? Are my elbows at an angle? How are my shoulders? Is my grip right? How is my backswing?"

"I see. We'll get to the backswing later. Let's take one thing at a time. So you see all of the aspects of your body as different parts?" Peter asked.

"Sure."

Peter paused for a moment. "I want you to try this. Think of all of the parts of your body aligned and working together, as one thing, almost like a car. When you turn the key it starts right up. That's because all the different parts act as one."

Jack understood what Peter was telling him intellectually, but physically his feet, hips, shoulders, arms, and grip were all separate things.

Peter could sense Jack was having difficulty and continued. "When you pour a glass of water, your hands are working in unison with your eyes, aiming for the glass, but you don't think of them as separate. You're acting as one."

"I think I see your point," Jack said, then paused for a second and really thought about it. "I guess in almost everything we do we take a lot of different actions and make them one thing, or else we couldn't do anything." Jack looked at Peter for his nod of approval.

"That's exactly right. Look at that man over there," Peter observed. Jack turned to watch a man older than Peter's 75 years hit a perfectly straight 250-yard drive. Peter continued, "He's in his eighties and barely swings but do you see how far the ball goes? It's because instead of using his arms, he's letting his body do the work. Everything is stacked, hips over feet, shoulders over hips, and head straight. No strenuous effort, and look at that ball go. That's because he's acting as one."

Jack nodded in understanding.

"So are you ready for another go?"

"Yes."

"So now when you swing again envision all of the different parts of your body stacked and acting as one."

Jack did as Peter said and simply swung.

"Good shot," Peter said as they heard a small click and watched the ball sail 110 yards straight in the air.

"How did that feel?" Peter asked.

"It felt good."

"Let's try it again. Envision everything stacked and acting as one."

Jack did as Peter said and again hit a perfectly straight shot, maybe 115 yards this time. He wondered, was this the sacrifice he'd have to make–distance for a straight drive?

"I know what you're thinking. Distance, am I right?" Peter asked.

"Well the thought did cross my mind. Should I try it again, but swing harder this time?"

"It's not about your arms moving harder or faster," Peter said. "Just as all of the parts of your body have to act as one for you to hit the ball straight, all of the aspects of your swing have to act as one to hit the ball a good distance."

Jack gave him a slightly puzzled look. What was Peter trying to get at?

"Just like pouring a glass of water. So what's the first part of your swing?" Peter asked.

"The backswing."

"Right, the backswing. And what's the next part of your swing?" Peter asked.

"The downswing."

"Right. So a slow backswing uncoils into a downswing and then you follow through. It's all one thing. Act as one."

"Act as one," Jack repeated.

"Exactly." Peter then paused and looked Jack in the eyes. "Just as your hips, shoulders, and arms are stacked and act as one, your backswing, downswing, and follow-through are stacked and act as one. It's that simple. Think of driving a car, think of pouring a glass of water. Now let's see you pour one 200 yards."

Jack did just as Peter instructed. As he swung down they heard a loud click and watched the ball sail 250 yards and perfectly straight.

"Well done! Remember, it's all one thing, like pouring a glass of water. Act as one."

For the rest of the afternoon Jack hit balls between 230 and 280 yards and straight.

Pour Me

As Jack drove to work Monday morning all he could think about were those 250-yard drives he made with Peter. Truth be told he wished he was going back to the driving range and not to his new job.

How was he going to reduce customer complaint response time? He put on a confident smile and told himself he'd do the best job he possibly could.

"Timothy, could you do me a favor and have the nursing department send up last week's customer complaint reports from radiology?" Jack asked.

"Sure thing, but sometimes it takes awhile."

"Why is that?"

"Truth is, there's a severe lack of communication between the nursing department and the radiology department," Timothy apologetically responded.

It seemed that the entire hospital was a group of departments at odds, just hoping not to be terminated.

Jack was having lunch in the employee lounge down the hall. He kept thinking how great it was to hear that loud click when he hit the ball dead on, then watch it fly over that beautiful green landscape.

"Oh excuse me, do you mind if I have my lunch here? It's a little crowded in the nurses' lounge."

"Please, have a seat." Jack smiled at the pleasant older woman in the nurse's outfit.

"Didn't I see you on 4D during the incident the other day with Mr. Seethers?" the nurse asked.

"As a matter of fact I was. Hi, my name's Jack, and I'm the new head of customer service." Jack stood up and politely extended his hand.

"Hello, Jack, my name's Maria and I'm a nurse here. Good luck with the new job."

"Thanks, Maria. I know your job is challenging. Anytime I can be of assistance, let me know."

"That's a first," Maria said with a casual smile.

"What's a first?" Jack asked with curiosity.

"Wanting to help. It seems like everyone at the hospital is out to undermine everyone else lately, and take credit anywhere they can get it," Maria said as she poured herself a large glass of bottled water.

"You're right. Forget being on the same page, no one's even reading the same book," Jack said, nodding in agreement.

Maria laughed as she took a large sip of water.

"One good thing about this kitchenette is it's always stocked with Poland Spring. Can I pour you a glass?" Maria asked in a nurturing manner that Jack assumed came from many years of nursing.

"Sure. Thank you, Maria."

As Jack watched Maria pour the glass of water he thought of his golf lesson with Peter and kept hearing Peter repeat in his deep, relaxed voice, "It's like pouring a glass of water. Act as one."

Jack drank the glass of water. Again he heard Peter's voice, "It's like pouring a glass of water. Act as one."

"Good, isn't it? I tell all my patients, my friends, my daughter, there's nothing like water. Here, let me pour you some more," Maria said as she refilled Jack's glass.

"Thanks again. And you're right, it is good."

And then, as Jack began to drink the second glass of water it hit him like a tidal wave. Peter's lesson applied to more than just his golf drive. If act as one was a way to cut through the confusion of golf, why couldn't he cut through the confusion and miscommunication at the hospital? The whole hospital should act as one! Every department is part of one thing, the hospital. Management and labor are part of one thing, the hospital. But everyone's so afraid of losing their jobs that they try to push the blame on another department or person.

People are probably spending half their time covering themselves. This is time that could be spent helping patients, which would increase referrals, which in turn would help the hospital.

It was all becoming crystal clear to Jack. The more time they spent helping patients, the more they connected with the purpose of their work, the better the hospital would run. Which would result in fewer complaints.

Reducing complaint response time was just playing not to lose. If they acted as one to enhance the patients' experience, they were playing to win. And everyone could win. The staff would help the customer, the customer would help the hospital, and the hospital would help the staff. So the more everyone acted as one, the less everyone would have to worry about job security.

"I was right, wasn't I? The water is good," Maria said with a kind maternal confidence.

"You don't know how right," Jack replied as he smiled and took a large gulp of water.

Business is Teaming

Jack met with Borchard, requesting a special meeting be set for that Friday for all departments to discuss how everyone at the hospital could work together more effectively to enhance customer service. And unlike many meetings just for department heads, everyone should be welcome to attend.

Friday came. After Bochard introduced Jack, he started the meeting by going around the room asking for people's ideas for improving customer service. One manager stressed the importance of reducing response time. A physician chimed in about everyone communicating more effectively with the patient. A nurse assistant talked about everyone working together to keep the patient's room clean. As several other ideas were brought up, Jack realized that it was beginning to happen. The hospital employees were acting more as one than they had before, even if it was agreeing on complaints. Jack then looked around the room of managers, nurses, doctors, executives, and other employees and prepared to present his new insight.

"We're all here, all of us, for the same purpose—the patients," Jack said. "We must all act as one. The work we do is of incredible importance. We all win as a team when we act as one. Everyone in the hospital from the doctors, to nurses, to housekeeping, to dietary, to transporting, to accounting, to my division customer service, is dependent on one other. It's that simple. We must all act as one."

Jack paused for a moment, to make sure everyone was following, then continued. "The more we think of ourselves as one thing, not separate, the better we'll all be. Let's all play to win, instead of just playing not to lose. The more we play as a team, the better the hospital will run, and equally important, the less everyone's job will be in jeopardy. We must all act as one every day."

"Well put Jack. Please continue," Bochard reinforced. Many people were nodding their heads in agreement. Others were just looking up, as if they didn't quite get it, or maybe they just didn't agree.

Then one of the managers stood up, waiting till he had everyone's attention, and said, "All this sounds good, but how do I ensure that my staff really understands what the actual strategy is?"

"You want to know how your staff understands what your actual strategy is?" Jack repeated, letting the question sink in, and giving himself a second longer to gauge his answer.

"Yes, how do they all understand what the strategy is?" the manager now repeated in a bolder voice.

"I'll tell you how your staff understands what your strategy is …" Jack paused for a long second. But up at the podium, in front of all those people, time slowed down.

Where was Jack going with this? Did he have an exact answer? Jack poured himself a glass of water to buy himself a few more seconds. For the first time in his career everyone was waiting on his words, and he wasn't sure what he was going to say. For a second Jack wondered if some good golf drives had given him a false sense of understanding and confidence.

Jack gulped down the rest of his glass of water. As he did he heard Peter's voice, "It's just like pouring a glass of water. Act as one." Great Jack thought. Here I am tongue-tied in front of all these people, and I'm hearing my golf pro's voice. Again Jack heard it. "Act as one."

And then the words just poured out of Jack's mouth. "Everyone understands the strategy because everyone plays a role in developing it," he said in a slightly muffled voice. Jack then repeated himself louder, clearer and slowly. "Everyone understands the strategy because everyone plays a role in developing it!"

There was a murmur among the audience, and everyone gazed at Jack with slightly puzzled looks.

"The whole point is that your team develops the strategy with you. It's not something that you dictate to them. Who would be better suited than the direct care workers to inform upper management about what actually takes place on each unit? And wouldn't those same staff members, who work with patients on a daily basis, be the best choice to help develop strategies that make the most sense for everyone? For too long it's been divided between management and staff. We must all act as one!"

People started nodding their heads in agreement. Jack

heard some of the managers turn to one another and repeat the words "act as one," as if to see if it made sense coming out of their mouths.

"I follow your point, but how specifically do we do it?" As Jack looked into the audience, he saw it was Maria, the nurse, who asked the question.

Jack paused, to give himself a second to think. Even though he was unsure of his next response, it reassured him to see Maria, who unknowingly helped him develop some of these new ideas.

Another manager stood up. "Yeah, I mean, theory is nice, but how does this actually work?"

OK, maybe Jack hadn't figured out all of the details. But he knew in his heart of hearts that to act as one made sense. He thought for another second, took a deep breath, looked out at everyone, and continued.

"Senior management must act as one and connect with doctors and staff. They must walk the halls to see what is actually going on. They must meet with our doctors and staff and ask them what they view our challenges to be, and how we could best solve them. We're all here for the same purpose, to help patients. We can never forget this. The patients are our customers. Their families are our customers," Jack said in his most urgent voice.

Another manager stood up. "But if staff is not happy, they won't provide good service."

"You're absolutely correct," Jack said, as he looked throughout the room and continued. "First we must inspire staff to be a real team. Everyone wants to be on a winning team, and every winning team has a common goal. We must all act as one and share that common goal."

"So what's the first step in creating a winning team?" a doctor asked from the back of the room.

"Yeah, where do we start?" Jack heard from somewhere in the middle of the room.

Jack digested the question and then continued. "When people work together on strategy, they build respect for each other and start acting as a team." He paused and looked out at all the managers and employees. "The first step in customer service is getting people to work together as a team. Teams are built by shared goals and respect for one another. When everyone has the same objectives they become a team." Jack saw many of the managers nod their heads, and continued. "All employees have a role, and teamwork mandates they first do their own job. Then they can pitch in and help others most effectively as teammates. Team doesn't start with getting help, it starts with helping others first."

"And what about the team's strategy towards the patient, or customer, as it is?" someone stood up and asked.

"Strategy, like any change, must start with the customer and their family."

"Sounds good, but what does that actually mean?" the same manager asked.

"For example, patients must view the hospital as one thing. For starters, they shouldn't have to register each time they change departments. They should just give their information once. And when they receive a bill, it should be

one simple-to-understand bill, not many confusing bills."
Jack looked out at everyone, reinforcing his message. "This
applies to clinical as well. Doctors and nurses, and nurse
assistants, must give the same answers about the patient's
care plan and procedures. This would apply to any business,
not just hospitals. And, after all, we are a business."

"So we're all on the same page," Jack heard someone
say.

"Exactly," Jack replied, pleased that people were
beginning to come together. He continued, "In great
hospitals, like all great organizations, everyone knows what's
going on throughout the organization. Communication is
essential."

More of the managers were now looking at Jack in
agreement. "For example, the staff stairway accumulates
trash that has clearly been dropped by the staff, since it is
not used by visitors. After we do our job, we must pick up
after one another. Create a level of excellence and respect
for our team."

"OK, but what about the problem of just too many
people in the Emergency Room?" a manager to Jack's
immediate right asked.

As Jack was thinking of a response, he heard Neil's
voice. "I think our problem is that we don't have enough
patients."

It occurred to Jack that Neil was right. The hospital had
to be open to as many patients as possible, and they all had
to act in agreement, and act as one on this. Jack hesitated
for a moment, knowing that if he said Neil was right, Neil

would somehow use it against him. But Jack knew he had to stick to his principles.

Jack looked directly at Neil and said, "You're exactly right. The more patients, the better it is for the hospital. We must all act as one on this common goal." As Jack said this he saw Neil give him a menacing smirk, like he had somehow gotten the best of him. It didn't matter to Jack; he knew he was doing the right thing for the hospital.

Then from the corner of his eye Jack saw the chief operating officer stand up.

"So I'm confused. Do we get staff to work as a team or to help develop the strategy?" the COO asked.

Jack paused. Everyone looked up at Jack. Time seemed to slow down for a moment.

"Yes," Jack answered.

"Yes?" asked the COO. "Which one?"

"Yes, both," Jack responded. "You see, by encouraging your staff members to come up with initiatives to improve customer service, they will be more likely to work together. Learning to work as a team will improve their communication, respect for each other, and morale. The result will be improved customer service. Labor and management will be working together as one. Two results—teamwork, and improved customer service. It's a self-sustaining cycle… happy staff provide better service, and satisfied customers promote employee pride."

The COO gave a small nod of approval, which for Jack was more than sufficient. After Jack finished, several people came up to him and said that they thought it was a very

motivational discussion that resonated strongly with them.
Others just walked out. Sure, Jack knew progress would be
slow. But it was a strong first step in the right direction.

After the meeting Jack wrote up and then e-mailed a list
of some simple things that all of the department heads
could do to ensure that people in their departments thought
and acted more as one unit. He added some specific actions
they could all do in their everyday jobs to think more as one
hospital, and not a collection of different jobs and
departments.

Act as One

1. **Get everyone involved and on the same team.**
   Staff and management work together to develop and
   implement strategy, gaining respect for one another as
   team members. All employees and departments work
   together as one team.

2. **Make sure everyone on the team has the same
   goal.**
   In sports, the goal is always clear and obvious—to win.
   In business, winning is not always easily defined. Thus
   any business should clearly define their goals that
   everyone on the team can share and follow. Once the
   goals are defined, the team must play to win.

3. **Give the team one face.**
   Create an environment where service throughout the
   organization is seamless to customers and to their
   families.

PART TWO

All for None and None for All

The meeting turned out to be a reasonable success. Jack received several e-mails from nurses, managers, doctors, and employees from numerous departments, praising his inspirational talk and relaying different stories of how some co-workers were developing and implementing strategies and discussing solutions and not just problems. Jack knew nothing happened overnight, but hoped that people would start to see that being on the same team could be less stressful, and more effective, than playing against one another. Jack knew some people saw him as too naïve, too enthusiastic, or just trying to secure his job. But that didn't get to him. Jack genuinely believed that to act as one made sense and that he had done the right thing.

The only negative response to the meeting was an e-mail Jack received from Neil, copied to all the other department managers and Bochard. In it Neil claimed that every department should act alone and compete against each other, which would ensure the survival of the fittest departments and the fittest workers.

This, Neil explained, would be the best way to weed out the weak links. If the hospital "acted as one," such pruning could never be accomplished. To Jack, act as one came from a place of strength and unity, but Neil made it sound like acting as one was for people or departments that couldn't stand on their own. Jack always thought that Neil was too scared to be a team player, but now he was making a logical argument for it. If Neil had his way the hospital would be a terror zone, with everyone battling for themselves.

Neil went on to write that although Jack delivered a nice speech it was numbers, not words, which made organizations work. He then reiterated Jack's words: "And as Jack said, this hospital is a business." He was trying to make it look like Jack missed the bigger picture.

Jack just hoped everyone understood that although competition might work for short-term numbers in the long run the patients, and ultimately the hospital, would lose.

Home Alone

Although Jack felt as though he'd won a small victory at work, things weren't going as well at home. The new job gave him even less time with Eve and Alex. Although Jack tried his best to leave the job at the hospital, it often came home with him. But as always, Eve patiently stood by his side, almost as if she knew something that Jack didn't. Although Jack was grateful for her support, he knew that even the strongest-willed people had their breaking point.

"So how are the golf lessons going?" Eve asked, knowing that golf was perhaps the only thing that wasn't stressful for Jack.

"Really good, actually. This Peter, the golf pro, is quite a character."

"Oh really. How so?"

"He just has this ancient wisdom way of explaining

things. He's like the Obi-Wan of golf, or something."

"Great. So now you can give up your golf clubs and just carry around a light saber," Eve said with a soft laugh.

A few years earlier Eve had switched from full time teaching substitute teaching, to spend more time with their daughter Alex. Jack had always felt it his privilege to be able to help facilitate this.

Jack and Eve shared a few more laughs that evening, but it never got deeper than that. Jack knew it had been some time since they really communicated, but he just had too much on his mind to go there. At least they weren't going backward, he rationalized.

What hurt Jack was that he knew how hard Eve tried to make things work for them, and that it was he who just hadn't been available emotionally.

In his den, Jack sat at his desk and studied the complaints. After a while he noticed certain patterns. For one thing, a majority of the complaints happened shortly after breakfast. A second thing was a majority of the complaints were lodged by a Mr. Bernie Seethers, at the standing rate of 19.3 a week. Jack remembered the irate Mr. Seethers from the week before.

Jack stared at the clock and tried to think of a possible connection to the complaints after breakfast and the Bernie Seethers enigma. He knew Eve wasn't crazy about him locking himself in the den again with a book of statistics. He also knew she was upset that he had missed Alex's ballet recital. Jack reasoned that, without a job, ballet classes might actually have to be cut. As he continued to stare at the clock, his mind began to ask questions. Was he really qualified for this new job? Was Eve, the best thing in his life, beginning to slip away from him? Was he becoming one of those fathers that he swore he'd never be, the kind that wasn't there?

Jack came to no realizations that night. In fact he fell asleep in his chair, only to wake up to the silence of the night and the loudness of his questions. As he walked into the bedroom he saw Eve sleeping. She looked so peaceful. So beautiful. He wondered if she was dreaming. And if so, about what? Silently Jack lay in bed beside Eve and watched her sleep.

A Fair Way

On Friday came a small relief. Customer complaints were actually down that week. Jack wasn't sure how much of it was due to his talk, his list of ideas, or luck; but he'd take any combination.

Jack e-mailed all of the department heads with the good news. He knew keeping up the momentum couldn't hurt.

Jack felt good and was looking forward to his second lesson with Peter.

"So with the drives you're hitting let's assume you're on the fairway," Peter said in his relaxed tone.

"Well, I can assume that you'd be on the fairway, but sometimes I wind up in the sand or deep in the rough," Jack jokingly replied.

Peter gave a knowing smile. "OK, let's assume you're in the sand. What's the most important thing, fairway or sand?"

"A good shot?" Somehow Jack knew there was to more to the answer.

"A good shot always helps, but more important is completing the circle."

"Completing the circle?" Jack repeated.

"That's right. Completing the circle means doing everything to make sure that the job gets done and you're on the green."

"You mean coming full circle, like on your swing?"

"Exactly. A golf swing is a circle. Just swing in a circular motion like you're going around a loop. That keeps you on the right plane. Then, when you do, you will complete the circle, to get on the green."

Peter sensed Jack's confusion and continued. "If you know you hit the 5 iron, 150 yards every time, the 6, 140, the 7, 130, even though you're not the longest hitter you'll create predictability and by completing the circle, get on the green."

"So you get on the green by completing the circle?" Jack asked, half repeating Peter's words to allow them to better sink in.

"That's right. Once you know your clubs, you just hit down on the ball and the ball will naturally go in the air because of the angle of the club. You let the club do the work. That's the club's purpose. The club is predictable and will complete the circle for you."

"But what if I hit off course, and get in a little trouble?" Jack couldn't help asking.

Peter politely smiled and said, "This sometimes happens and the same rule applies. Complete the circle."

"How?"

"Take the stroke and get out of trouble immediately. Create predictability and complete the circle. Don't try to be a hero, you'll lose more in the long run."

"Is that how you escape the problem?"

Peter chuckled. "Unfortunately there's only one way to escape a problem."

"One way? I thought there were many ways to escape a problem," Jack said, looking at Peter.

"The only way to escape a problem …"–Jack hung on Peter's last syllable as he paused for a long second–"is solve the problem. Face reality… and solve the problem. And the way to solve your problem is to create predictability by completing the circle."

"I think I understand, but how do you ensure you complete the circle?"

"Good question." Peter again paused. "The way to complete the circle is through predictable routine. You see what works and what doesn't work, and you do the things that work, over and over again. You practice your swing over and over again. This creates muscle memory. You then visualize hitting your shot over and over again, until you are in the habit of creating predictability and completing the circle every time. Some people call this getting in the zone."

The Good Nurse

Back in his office, Jack wondered, was there any connection between Mr. Seethers and the complaint time? The only connection Jack could see was that Mr. Seethers also complained right after breakfast. Unless Seethers and other patients were all complaining about indigestion from a bad breakfast, Jack couldn't see the connection.

As he sat back at his desk and thought, Jack smiled at an e-mail he received from Maria the nurse he had met in the kitchenette.

She wrote:

Hello Jack,

Just wanted you to know that since your meeting the nurses and their assistants have become friendlier, and now many even sit together during their 9:00AM break.

Jack quickly responded, thanking Maria for the e-mail. He realized that the quick response was a sign of courtesy, which people really liked. Ah, Jack thought, he was creating predictability and completing the circle by confirming that he received the e-mail. Peter was beginning to seem more like a master of business than a golf pro.

Jack decided to walk down to the nurse's station and

take a first-hand look. And while he was there he'd pay a
visit to Maria and thank her in person.

On his way down Jack noticed something that brought
a smile to his face. He witnessed a transporter involved in a
great conversation with the patient he was transporting.

"Since I'm the last person I just wanted to make sure
your stay was very good." Jack overheard.

Both were smiling and he could see the care in both the
transporter's and the patient's eyes. Was it Jack's
imagination or was his little speech beginning to yield small
victories?

Then a little later Jack was watching the nurses and
assistants all have coffee together. He could see the
camaraderie. But wait, he thought. No wonder all the
complaints came shortly after 9AM – the entire staff was on
a break.

"Maybe we could stagger the breaks so we have even
number of staff on the units to ensure appropriate
coverage." Jack suggested to Maria.

"You do have a point. I'll ask the nurse manager and see
what she thinks."

"Also if someone could check on Mr. Seethers regularly
at 9:15 I think we'd solve our biggest customer complaint."

As it turned out, Maria was right. A lot of the nurses
were happy to change break time to balance coverage. The
staff also agreed to give Mr. Seethers a regular check at 9:15,
problem or not.

Within two weeks after Jack met with Maria, customer

complaints went down even more. Jack smiled. He sent an e-mail to the chief operating officer, reporting the progress of the nursing staff. It was actually working, he thought— they were creating predictability and completing the circle.

Since he was on a roll, he decided to do a little checking of his own, and see if there weren't some other ways of completing the circle.

Jack waited quietly near Bernie Seethers's room; it was time for his medication. A few minutes later a nurse walked into his room, administered his medication, and then went to wash her hands.

As she was washing her hands, Mr. Seethers said, "Thank you, nurse."

"You're welcome, not a problem," the nurse said as she dried her hands, smiled, and left the room.

Two things occurred to Jack. One was that Bernie Seethers didn't appear to be as obstreperous as all the reports made him out to be, and two was that the nurse did nothing particularly wrong.

Jack decided to spend a little more time getting a feel for patient care. A few doors down he stopped and watched as a different nurse entered an elderly patient's room.

"Hi. My name is Wanda Jones. I am your nurse today and I will be administering your medication," the nurse said with a smile.

As the man smiled back, the nurse sat down beside him, looked him in the eyes, and continued, "Mr. Eldron, I understand that you've been having a lot of pain in your left knee, and that the last medication you received disturbed your stomach. This one should solve both problems." She washed her hands and then administered the medication.

She said, "I want to thank you, Mr. Eldron, for being so brave. I know that must have hurt. You really are a real trooper" She then smiled at him with shining eyes.

Mr. Eldron's face lit up as he said, "Thank you so much for your concern."

Finally, the nurse said, "I'll try to be back before 10:30 AM. Have a great day!"

"You have a great day Ms. Jones!" Mr. Eldron said cheerfully.

Jack decided to follow the second nurse and see how her bedside manner worked with other patients. After she administered medication with two more patients the exact same way, Jack got it. The second nurse administered the same medication as the first, but it was a totally different experience for her patients. And it took the same amount of time as the first nurse. She was finishing every part of the interaction and the job by completing the circle. Completing the circle meant leaving nothing to chance.

Jack then thought if the hospital could document these processes and communicate them, it would ensure positive, predictable outcomes.

Complete the Circle

1. Do your job the same way every time to create predictability.

2. Complete every element of your work, from customer discussions to job specifics.

3. **Never let anything get out of control.** If small problems are attended to, they will not become bigger problems.

Brand New Circle

Jack realized that most successful businesses, from service to retail, from selling a car to selling ideas, create predictable outcomes and complete the circle–whether it's a thank-you first or a standard warm greeting. The Starbucks organization was a good example. They would greet him the same way at any franchise in any city. They completed the circle. They branded themselves, as any successful organization must do.

Jack later went to Maria to discuss what he'd witnessed. "Completing the circle means we do what our advertising says. It's that simple. A hospital is supposed to take care of its patients, just as any business must take care of its customers."

"Jack, you're exactly right. Although I knew this intuitively, I hadn't acted on it. I will ask our nurse manager to set up a meeting where we all as a team can come up with a list of predictable standards that nurses could follow to complete the circle. This will definitely make our jobs easier and more effective. It will also solve many problems before they arise. And once we achieve results, as well as a lightened load from more effective patient interactions, I bet it will spread."

"That's great. Thank you, Maria," Jack said.

Maria smiled kindly at Jack. "I'll tell you one other thing I've learned throughout my 30 years at the hospital. If you spend a few moments longer to create an initial warm rapport with a patient, all of your future interactions will be filtered through the positive lens of that first meeting. Everyone's good side will come out naturally. All of your interactions will become easier, more pleasant, and more energizing for both parties."

"Wow, that's a very interesting way to complete the circle, Maria. You're beginning to sound like my golf pro," Jack said lightly, pretty sure that she'd have no idea what he was talking about.

"Oh, do you play? What's your handicap?" Maria asked, not missing a beat.

"Well, I'm still just a notch above hacker but I started taking lessons, and I've learned that some of the lessons apply to business as well."

"I agree, Jack. Another thing I've noticed is that a lot of businessmen say they golf because it's a good opportunity for building relationships, when really they are addicted to the experience of having their mind focused on a single object, that little white ball."

"I think you're exactly right," Jack agreed.

"I think as a rule of thumb in work the mind is irritated moving from one thought to another, and there is something about completely focusing on one object that puts the mind at ease," Maria said, seemingly pleased that she had a new friend that she could share her golf revelations with.

"We should play sometime. It will be my treat. I think I could learn a thing or two from you."

"I'd love to, but be forewarned: I'm a seven handicap," Maria said with her biggest grin of all.

The next week Maria e-mailed a list of standards that the nursing staff had all contributed to making together. They jokingly called them the Ten Commandments.

The Ten Commandments of Completing the Circle

1. Create an initial warm rapport with the customer so all future interactions will be filtered through this first impression.

2. Completely understand the customer's needs. Find out particulars of what the customer really wants. Confirm with the customer that they received what they wanted.

3. Complete the service. This means that the customer must clearly understand any future steps that will be taken, i.e. medications, procedures.

4. Say "Thank you" first. This completes the communication circle. Every time we say, "You're welcome," the customer–not us–has completed the circle.

5. Listen to all complaints, try to resolve the problem and prevent reoccurrence. Then explain back to the customer what you have done.

6. Complete your work. Leave nothing undone.

7. Communicate to the person who assigned the job that it's completed. And when people speak, let them know you've heard and understand what they've said.

8. Put everything back in its proper place immediately so everything's always where it should be; return what you borrow and clean up after yourself.

9. When a co-worker is having a tough day, offer to help them out. When you are having a rough day, reach out to co-workers for their support. Develop a positive working relationship with every person on your team.

10. By completing the circle every time, nothing will get out of your control.

PART THREE

The Next Front

"Jack, we have to talk. Meet me in fifteen minutes in the coffee shop. It's important," urged Timothy.

Jack wondered what could be so urgent that Timothy couldn't just tell him in the customer service office.

Jack went down to the coffee shop and met Timothy. "Neil is plotting against us. He's trying to find a legitimate way to get rid of people in the customer service department." Timothy quickly paused as a doctor passed them.

Timothy continued, "I noticed he's been sending a lot of private e-mails. I think he wants to be head of accounting, and figures the job could be his if he can single-handedly ax some jobs and cut costs. Mine and yours being the first. I can't afford to lose my job, Jack. I've been here too long. But that's probably what makes me look bad, right?" Timothy nervously asked.

"Don't worry, Timothy. You're good at your job, and you're a team player. You're not going anywhere. Thanks for bringing this to my attention, but don't let it get to you," Jack said reassuringly.

"Are you sure?"

"Timothy, we're going to do our best and stick to doing the right thing," Jack said, smiling at Timothy and giving him a firm pat on the shoulder.

As Jack drove home, his mind began to wander. He wondered what would happen to the hospital and its patients if Neil was successful in dismantling the customer service department. The more Jack thought about it, the more concerned he became with the Neil issue. The only thing Jack was sure about was that he wasn't going to let his teammates down, and that he was going to do his job and what was best for the hospital. As Jack opened the door to his house he knew he had to find an answer.

"Daddy, Daddy, look at the picture I drew in school today." Alex ran up to Jack as he opened the door.

"Looks great, sweetie," Jack said as he headed directly for the den. Jack felt bad that he couldn't give his daughter more attention, but he just had too much on his plate.

As Jack ate dinner, Eve could tell he wasn't listening to a word she was saying. This Neil issue was getting to him.

"You look like you have a lot on your mind. Why don't you skip dessert? We can talk later," Eve said to Jack.

"I'm sorry, honey, do you want to talk?"

"No, it's fine, you get your work finished."

"We'll talk later. There's just something's that I need to figure out."

"Too bad Peter the golf guru isn't around to help you." Jack stared at Eve in surprise—she wasn't usually sarcastic.

"Don't worry, it's fine, really." As Eve spoke, she quickly, and with no emotion, kissed Jack on the forehead, collected his plate, and took it into the kitchen.

Jack knew what Eve was thinking. She'd heard the "we'll talk later" line too many times. For the first time it occurred to Jack that maybe Eve was pulling away from him. Maybe she was just going through the motions, as she might have thought he was. Maybe she was beginning to give up on them.

The Green

A couple of weeks had passed since Jack met with Timothy in the coffee shop. The only solution Jack could come up with to combat Neil was to continue improving customer service. Don't play to not lose. Play to win.

Jack was looking forward to his last lesson with Peter. Putting was a lesson of extreme importance. After all, if you hit a beautiful 250-yard drive, and got on the green with an amazingly accurate chip, but it took three strokes to sink the ball, you still had to add those three strokes.

"Now, tell me what you know about putting," Peter said in his usual relaxed tone.

Jack thought for a second before answering, knowing that whatever he said, Peter would probably have a simpler and more profound response.

"Well, I know if you miss a putt by one inch, it's the equivalent of a terrible drive. I know putting is like a pendulum action, where you move your shoulders but not your hands. I know not to bring my putter back too far, and to follow through."

"Very good. Now I'm going to teach you one other thing. It's called the U factor. Before you do anything else, you want to study the green, and <u>uncover</u> what is <u>unique</u> about it. Is there anything unique about this green?" Peter asked.

As Jack looked, he noticed that it sloped slightly to the left.

"Yes, it slopes ever so slightly to the left."

"Exactly. That is the <u>undulation</u> of the green. So whenever you're on a green, you have to study what is unique about its undulations. This lets you <u>understand</u> the green. Do you follow?" Peter asked, knowing he had given Jack a mindful.

"Find the U factor. Which is uncovering what is unique about the undulations of the green, so you can better understand the green," Jack repeated, letting it sink in.

"Yes. And once you understand the green, you'll know how to best play it," Peter said with his relaxed smile. "In fact, strong players will not just try to get on the green. They're always aiming for a particular part of the green where, depending on where the pin is placed, the unique undulations will make the putt easier. And when someone chips or putts before them, they study the exact slopes and undulations so they understand the best way to approach the hole."

Peter and Jack went to the greens of all 18 holes on the course. Peter was right. Each green was unique, with different undulations. Once you understood these unique undulations, the U factor, you would know how to best play the hole. Not that Jack mastered the art of putting. Peter explained that even he often missed what appeared to be an easy putt. And that's why golf was golf.

All That Jazz

Jack was already thinking how he could apply the U factor to customer service as he headed to work. He had a sneaking suspicion there could be a way.

As he read the customer complaints for the last week, he noticed there were fewer, but there had to be a way to bring them down even more. Could the U factor help?

That was it! Jack called his good friend Maria and asked her if she could find anything unique about Mr. Seethers.

"What do you mean, unique, he's been in and out of the hospital more times than most over the past few months. Other than that fact, the only thing unique is that he complains a lot." Maria asked, with a smile that Jack could almost see even over the phone.

"Any unique hobbies, likes, dislikes, that could help us to better understand him," Jack said, hoping Maria would understand.

"I think I know what you're driving at. I'll see what I can find out and get back to you."

"Thanks, Maria, you're the best, and I'm still preparing for our golf outing," Jack said with his own smile that he hoped came through over the phone.

A few hours later Maria called Jack. The only thing she could find out was that Bernie Seethers liked Dixieland jazz.

At lunchtime Jack went to Tower Records and bought a compilation CD, the Best of Dixieland. That afternoon Jack went to Mr. Seethers's room with a portable CD player he had borrowed from the custodial staff, and the CD he had bought.

"Hello, Mr. Seethers," Jack politely said as he entered his room.

"Yes, what is it?" Mr. Seethers replied in a voice that was more sad than agitated.

"Hello, my name is Jack. I am the head of customer service, and I heard that you like Dixieland jazz so I bought this CD. Do you mind if I play it?"

Mr. Seethers's face lit up. It was as if Jack told him he was cured, and had won the lottery.

"Dixieland ... I didn't know anyone listened to it anymore. It's been such a long time."

As Jack handed him the CD, he sat up in the bed, put his reading glasses on, and studied it intensely.

"Good stuff. Can you play track four?" he asked.

"Sure thing."

As Jack plugged in the portable CD player and played track four, he saw a revelation before his eyes. Mr. Seethers wore a look of contentment that one rarely sees from a hospital patient.

"Tin Roof Blues ... that was always my favorite," he said, smiling.

Then Mr. Seethers did the weirdest thing. He actually started mimicking the sound of a trombone with his mouth, and moved his right hand as if he were playing a real trombone. He played right along with the record. Not only that, he was actually good.

Jack and Mr. Seethers talked for over an hour that day. He told Jack how he always wanted to be a jazz musician and used to sneak into jazz clubs when he was a kid. He was a very entertaining storyteller. By the end of the hour Mr. Seethers had attracted a fan base of two custodians. Although they initially came to retrieve their CD player, after they listened to Seethers mouthing the trombone, they said he could hold on to it for a while.

The next week Jack received an e-mail from Maria. Not only had Mr. Seethers stopped lodging complaints, he now regularly entertained the nurses and custodians with his "Tin Roof Blues" trombone.

Maria then wrote something that stopped Jack right in his tracks. It turned out that a seven-year-old girl, Jenny Heartman, diagnosed with cancer, was being hospitalized in the adjacent unit, just four rooms down from Bernie Seethers. She had asked the nurse where the music was coming from because she liked it. So they wanted to bring Jenny Heartman to Bernie Seethers's room at three o'clock that afternoon, and Maria asked if Jack could be there.

It was five minutes before three o'clock and Bernie Seethers couldn't be in a better mood as he talked to Jack.

"Sure I was a regular at Eddie Condon's, best jazz club in New York. Everyone–Coltrane, Miles, Dizzy–came down to play. Every night was a happening. But I'll tell ya sumthin', kid, none of them could touch Dixieland jazz. That was the birth and the jewel of the jazz world. I'll tell ya, since you got me that CD, I've been a changed man. But when I heard about what happened in New Orleans, that broke my heart. Louie Armstrong, Jelly Roll Morton, all from New Orleans–it makes you realize every day of life is a gift."

"I think you're right, Mr. Seethers. Unfortunately sometimes we forget it, or take it for granted," Jack said with a warm smile.

"First off, it's Bernie, and second you're right. We do take the gift for granted, and even as sick as I am, it's a gift. And the gift is the present. Get it, the present." Bernie then let out a gruff, contagious laugh.

"Speaking of gifts, I have a request I'd like to ask you, Bernie."

"Shoot, kid," Bernie said as he jokingly cocked his thumb and forefinger.

"Well, there is a seven-year-old girl, Jenny Heartman, who has cancer, and she's temporarily staying one unit over on this floor a few doors down, since she has to make so many visits to radiation therapy."

"Oh, I see," Bernie said with a changed tone of genuine concern.

"Well, it seems that she heard you doing your trombone, and … well … she rather liked it."

Bernie's face lit up with a look that could best be described as enlightened.

He was listening intently. Jack continued, "If it's all right with you, we were going to bring her by. We thought it might cheer her up a bit."

Bernie had a moment of extreme emotion, as if pondering the weight of what had just been requested.

"Excuse me," a nurse said from outside Bernie's door, "is it all right if we come in?"

Bernie nodded a yes to Jack.

"Sure, please do. I'm Jack, and this is Bernie," Jack said with a soft smile as the nurse wheeled in seven-year-old Jenny. Apart from the wheelchair and baseball hat, she looked like any other pretty little seven-year-old girl. She had big green eyes, a little turned-up nose, and a missing front tooth.

"Hello," Jenny said shyly, looking at Jack and Bernie.

Jack felt a little awkward and thought that perhaps they had made a mistake by bringing together this fragile young girl and this recently reformed grumpy old man.

"Why, hello there, Jenny. What a pleasure it is to meet you. You remind me of my daughter when she was your age, but I think you're actually a little prettier than she was, and she was quite pretty," Bernie said with a beaming smile that took all the awkwardness out of the room in an instant. Bernie took over; he was in performance mode.

"So I hear you want to learn how to do what I call the human trombone," Bernie said with a smile and a little wink.

"Yes, I liked the way it sounded the other day," Jenny said, beginning to relax.

"Maestro, if you will." Bernie pointed to the portable CD player, indicating Jack should start the show.

"You know, Jenny, your timing is really perfect. I was just asking Jack if he knew anyone with a missing tooth, to play trombone with me, since that missing tooth gives it a muted sound effect. And here you are … go figure."

Jenny let out a little giggle.

"There you go. Well, we're going to have some fun. First you have to form your mouth into a sort of circle, and then we have to find your tone." Bernie went on as he showed her how to form her mouth to get the best sound.

For the next hour Jack quietly sat there mesmerized as the little girl laughed, and had so much fun mimicking the trombone to the music with the old man. Bernie Seethers had a renewed purpose in life.

As it came time for Jenny to leave, they made plans for her to come by for some more Tin Roof Blues. Jack sat in awe of one of the most rewarding and unexpected days he'd had since he worked at the hospital. Neil aside, Jack's job aside, they had uncovered a small, unique miracle.

It really hit Jack later. If they could just find some simple things that were unique about their patients, they could better understand and care for them. Probably not in any way nearly as profound as Bernie and Jenny's connection, but it was about uncovering those unique undulations.

The next day Jack went down to thank Maria. Again she had helped create magic.

"Well, you're quite welcome, but to be honest I'm just as surprised as you. Jenny's mother kept me on the phone for over 10 minutes. She was just so thrilled. And, as it turns out, Bernie had lost his daughter several years back, so now he has a surrogate daughter and granddaughter. Jack, I think your golf guru is the one who really worked the magic," Maria said with a broad grin. Jack just nodded his head.

"I actually have asked my staff to make a habit of inquiring how patients uniquely want to be treated—things like pain medication, amount of interactions, whether they like talking or being quiet. And I really feel it's beginning to make a difference in how we can best serve the patients. Hey, I know a lot of the nurses are trying to not make a mistake for fear of losing their license, but the more tools we give them, the less they'll fear losing their jobs. The more we implement these standards, the more they'll feel in control of their situation. It's all about uncovering what's unique, which is a strength, never a weakness."

"My golf guru calls this the U factor. Uncover Unique Undulations to better Understand."

"The U factor, I like that. Let me guess—your guru took you putting," Maria said with a small laugh.

Jack laughed and Maria joined in.

"Now is that a capital U, or y-o-u, or both?" Maria added with a smile.

"I like that. Maybe the fifth U is be yourself."

Maria nodded in agreement.

"Thank you, Maria. Every time I have some enthusiastic vision, you have a way of making it tangible, and making it work for the hospital. You really make this institution a special place. I'm thankful for people like you," Jack said as sincerely as he possibly could.

"Well, to be honest, at first I thought the principle of

uncovering uniqueness and completing the circle with predictability were opposed, but they're not. All we have to do is combine all the predictable procedures that patients want with their unique interests. That's when we really do right by our customers."

"You're right. They really do go together perfectly," Jack said as he listened to Maria's natural way of putting things.

"We're all in this together, right? Acting as one, creating predictability and completing the circle, uncovering what's unique so we can really understand."

"I couldn't have said it better myself," Jack said, giving a look of sincere appreciation.

"Actually those were your words, Jack, but you'll make it up to me on the golf course."

As Jack left Maria's nursing area, it occurred to him that they also had to find out what was unique about each staff member. Every person has a unique combination of skills, abilities, and passions. If we understand these, they can be not just managed but genuinely inspired. Then we could find what is unique about our organization to uncover its true strength. Which again led Jack to the final U in the U factor. For every person and institution to be their best, be yourself.

A little bit later while Jack was walking to his car, one unique fact jumped out at him. The community that the hospital served had one of the highest birthrates of any community in the region.

Jack immediately sent an e-mail to all the department

heads and nursing staff: Find out what was unique about their patients and employees. Customer service was really all about creating positive experiences. Was there anything specific that could help make their hospital experience a positive one? Then Jack mentioned the unique fact of high birthrates in their community. Perhaps they could cater to this unique undulation in the community with an increased or specialized maternity ward. After all, what better way to increase customers than providing for the whole family?

The U Factor

1. **Uncover, Uniqueness, Undulations, Understanding**

    Find out something unique about each customer (and staff member). Know their stories.

2. **Find out what style of interaction, and specifics would make the relationship more positive.**

3. **Be YOURSELF.** Share of yourself to build a genuine relationship with the customer.

PART FOUR

Be the Course

As Jack thought about the upcoming quarterly meeting, he was feeling pretty good about things. Customer complaints were down and Bernie and Jenny regularly jammed the Tin Roof Blues.

Jack felt confident as he headed to the golf course. Although his lessons with Peter were over, Peter invited Jack to play the course with him, as a friend.

"Nice putt," Peter calmly said as Jack sank a 17-foot putt on the fourth hole.

"Thank you, Peter. I can't tell you how much I owe you. You have no idea how much these lessons meant to me."

"You don't owe me a thing. It was my pleasure. Just remember to always have respect for the game, the players, and the course."

"I will," Jack answered. Throughout their lessons Peter would always talk of etiquette—to clear your footprints from the sand, to repair your divots, where to stand so as not to distract other golfers. All were lessons to which Jack paid close attention.

"Top golfers take pride in leaving the course in better shape than when they got there," Peter said with the pride of a top golfer.

The analogy occurred to Jack immediately. People in any organization could exhibit the same type of etiquette and respect, whether it's throwing out garbage in the employee lounge or making sure you get people the appropriate information at the appropriate time.

"Remember … be the course," Peter said in that profound way Jack had become accustomed to.

"Be the course. What do you mean?"

"I mean when you respect the game, you become a part of its history, its legacy. You become part of something bigger than yourself. Golf has been around before you and will be around after you. Have respect for that."

Jack nodded his head in appreciation. It then sank in that "being the course" applied to every institution, job, or team. They're all part of something bigger than themselves.

As Jack was ready to drive the last hole of the day, Peter looked at him, seeming to review the progress he had made since he first came to him.

"Now I know how much you learned through these lessons. You really have been a remarkable student and it's been my pleasure to share some of the lessons I've learned. So here is the last thing I will tell you."

As Jack leaned in, he wondered. Could this be the final revelation that could change him? He patiently waited, as Peter looked up at the sky, as if it was Moses ready to give him the last Commandment. Peter again looked at Jack.

"Always remember, this sounds simple, but it's really the whole thing of golf." Peter again paused for a few seconds.

Then Peter pointed to the ball on the tee and slowly said, "The show's right here."

"The show's right here," Jack repeated. Weren't those

the exact words that had lost Jack the match with Ted those months back, when he first saw Peter? Jack made a conscious effort to completely focus and try to understand the exact meaning.

"Keep your eye right where the show is. The show's not over there, two hundred yards away. The show's not at the next hole, or the hole after that. The show's not in the trees, or in the water. The show's not where you will be in three hours, or three days from now. The show's right here in front of you, and it's always waiting for you to begin. If you did everything right, you'll make your shot."

Jack nodded. "I understand. Let me ask you, does this tie into the other lessons we learned–you know, act as one, complete the circle, the U factor?"

"It sure does. It's the culmination of everything you've learned."

Jack gave Peter a slightly puzzled look, which he knew Peter had become accustomed to.

"What I really mean is that all of these lessons I've taught you apply to more than just golf," Peter calmly added.

Could Peter know how Jack had applied all of the golf lessons to work? How, he thought?

"You mean it could apply to business?" Jack asked.

"Sure, it could apply to anything, business, sports … anything. I know golf seems like an individual sport but pick a team sport."

"Basketball," Jack quickly answered, knowing that

nothing could be a further sport from golf than basketball.

"OK, basketball. Now first you have to make everyone feel that they're on the same team with the same goal and one face, right?" Peter asked as he looked at Jack.

"Right."

"Then next, at whatever level you're at–whether it's high school or pro–you create predictability and complete the circle by practicing lay-ups, free-throws, passing, so when the game's on the line your team has the best chance for a positive outcome, right?"

"Right."

"Well then, you have to know your U factor. Really uncover what's unique about your players to know your team. Understand their undulations. Are they big and slow or small and quick? Are they best at shooting the outside shot or strong on defense? Surely you won't play a five-foot-five guard the same way you'd play a seven-foot center, right?"

"OK, I think I see your point," Jack said.

"You make uniqueness work for you. I've seen teams that didn't have the greatest offense make the other team lose because they played great defense. And now this is when it all comes together–after the team has one goal, practices to create predictability and complete the circle, and uncovers its uniqueness. Then it's game time. The show's right here. For those forty-eight minutes, or however long, you and your team have to be in that moment. It's the same for any other team or business."

"For any business?" Jack repeated, thinking it couldn't

possibly apply to all businesses.

"Sure, pick any business."

"OK, how about a restaurant?"

"A restaurant." Peter paused and thought for a second. "Well, first the restaurant must be seen as one entity, with a shared understanding of what their brand of the customer experience should be. Then they must train their employees to create predictable outcomes, hopefully great food, to complete the circle. They must also understand–from hostess, to waiter, to cook, to chef–everyone's unique role. Then when it's time for business, the whole team must remember that the show is right here, in that moment."

Again Jack nodded, letting Peter know it all made sense.

"Here's the thing you should really remember, though," Peter said as he gave Jack a warm and sincere look. "Not only do these rules apply to golf and business, they apply to your entire life. Your personal relationships, your family, your friends. Everything."

As Jack left Peter, he felt enlightened, in an almost spiritual way. How fortunate he was to find him, he thought. How fortunate he was to enjoy even a minute of "the show" with him.

The Showdown

As Jack headed into the hospital meeting, he felt good that he was part of the legacy of the hospital that was bigger than any individual or department. They were all part of something, helping others, that was bigger than themselves.

Since Jack had first met Peter, his thinking had evolved. At first he was concerned about his job and how to handle and respond to complaints more efficiently. Now he was concerned about the hospital, and realized the right approach was to correct problems before they ever happened. That's how the hospital and everyone in the hospital could best live up to their part of the hospital's history and legacy.

You could hear a pin drop in the room as Bochard concluded her opening report. "And so, all in all, we've had a good quarter." All of the department heads and workers clapped loudly.

"Would anyone like to add anything?" Ms. Bochard asked as she looked out into the audience of Jack's fellow workers.

There was a relaxed silence throughout the room, and then Jack heard it.

"Yes, I would." Before Jack turned around, he recognized Neil's voice.

Jack straightened out his shoulders and prepared himself for Neil's inevitable attack.

"Yes, please go ahead," answered Bochard.

Neil stood up, and then took a long second to make sure he had everyone's attention.

"Yes, while going through records, I realized that there were some discrepancies, and that some departments don't appear to be holding their own very well."

The room was silent, as everyone wondered where the

attack was headed. Jack knew where it was headed. Jack also knew he'd been doing the right thing and was prepared to stand by all of his actions.

"Please continue," Bochard said, offering Neil what seemed to be an unusual amount of respect.

"Thank you, Ms. Bochard," Neil said, and politely nodded.

"Yes. Well, it appears that one patient, Mr. Seethers, has single-handedly lodged 83 complaints," Neil said, then paused knowing he had gotten everyone's undivided attention.

Jack heard small murmurs throughout the crowd, and then immediately felt everyone's eyes on him. Although he knew that Bernie Seethers hadn't lodged a complaint for a few weeks, he wondered if the turnaround wasn't too little too late.

"Well, I took it upon myself to see if Mr. Seethers could be transferred to another hospital, and found out that under his current insurance he would be allowed to. This move would not only lower the general number of customer complaints but it would also save the hospital money because we wouldn't need so many resources to handle his complaints. And, since Medicare pays us only for a certain number of days, each time he stays longer we lose money." Neil said with the authority of someone explaining a revelation. The murmurs in the crowd increased, and now all eyes were intently focused on Jack.

"It appears to me that apart from the customer service department not living up to its duties, this single gross inefficiency further exemplifies why the six-person customer service department should not only be cut, but completely torn down and reformed."

Everyone was completely silent. Jack saw Bochard look directly at him. As Jack stared back at her, he wondered if this was his final stand? Did Bochard let Neil do her dirty work? If so, Jack was going to stick by what he believed in. But more than himself, it was what he believed was right for the organization, all of its employees, and all of the customers they served. Jack wasn't going to let the people who believed in him down without a fight, even if it meant losing his job.

As Jack stood there, he heard Peter's words, "The show's right here. The show's right here." Jack then stepped forward and calmly but forcefully said, "Though this may be true, I think it is extremely important to the hospital as an institution that we do not turn our backs on any problem that we cannot handle, that it is our duty, that it is our job." Everyone stood silent as Jack paused for a long second and looked around the room. He continued, "But most of all it is our privilege to gain the respect and trust of all of our customers, regardless of the situation."

As Jack said this, he knew that by standing by his beliefs he could put his head on the pillow at night, even if it was a chopped head. There was a moment of silence, then Jack heard Neil's voice.

"I'm sorry if you've forgotten, but this hospital is a business. I'm in accounting so I know this. As a matter of fact, in your big meeting, I believe you said it was a business too. Perhaps this just slipped your mind."

Jack shot back, "Yes, it is a business. A business of helping people!"

"It appears that you don't see the numbers. Perhaps I should explain them more clearly," Neil said, looking directly at Bochard.

As Jack looked directly at Neil and then Bochard, it happened. Bochard spoke. "I think this topic can wait until …"

Neil interrupted, "Excuse me, Ms. Bochard, if I could just finish, I wanted to show the numbers more clearly …"

Ms. Bochard interrupted Neil, "Please have a seat."

"But if I could …" Neil tried to continue.

"A seat, please," Bochard sternly retorted.

After Neil took his seat, Bochard continued. "First of all, I agree with Jack, we must be part of something bigger than ourselves, and numbers do not always tell the whole story. Unfortunately we lost one of our patients last night. At approximately two AM Mr. Bernie Seethers passed away. While it is true Mr. Seethers had lodged more complaints than any other patient in this hospital's history, it is also true that he had not lodged a single complaint during the last weeks of his life. It is further true that he forged a unique friendship with a seven-year-old cancer patient, Jenny Heartman, who has now gone into partial remission." Jack could hear the surprised murmurs travel throughout the room. Ms. Bochard waited a few seconds, then continued.

"Two days ago Bernie Seethers redirected his will and testament. It appears Bernie Seethers rather enjoyed the last few weeks of his life and stay here, and his special bond with Jenny Heartman. So much in fact that he instructed his lawyer if something were to happen to him to call me immediately to tell me that he had left a gift." Everyone in the room was listening intently.

Bochard continued, "A gift of two million dollars to the hospital to spend in any way we saw fit." As Bochard said this with a huge grin on her face, everyone in the room rose to their feet and gave a loud round of applause.

Bochard continued, "We at the hospital are very grateful for his generosity, but more importantly, we should all be proud that we made the last few weeks of his life as enjoyable as possible. Remember, our mission at the hospital is to save lives, help lives, and help people. And although I am deeply saddened that we lost a patient today, I am equally proud that we made his last weeks as pleasant as we possibly could. And for that, I would like to thank you all."

Again there was a large round of applause.

"Oh, and one other thing, it has been brought to my attention that the community that this hospital serves yields a significantly higher than average birth rate. So I thought a good way to increase customer service and plan for the hospital's future would be to use Mr. Seethers' gift to expand our maternity ward and create customers for life, because families are the future of this hospital. His lawyer believes that he would have been very happy with this decision. Once again, thank you all."

A huge round of applause filled the room. As a huge grin filled Jack's face, he realized one thing. The show is right here. And what a show it was!

The Show

Jack drove home stunned. Who would have guessed that Bernie Seethers would do such a thing, or that he had that much money? He couldn't wait to tell Eve the news.

Alex greeted him at the door, shouting, "Daddy, Daddy, look at the picture I drew in class today!"

As Jack kissed Alex and headed toward the kitchen, he said, "Very good, very good, sweetie."

As Jack entered the kitchen, he turned around and stopped. Why was he rushing, and what was he rushing to? This was his beautiful daughter whom he'd neglected because he was consumed with work, and yet she still loved him unconditionally, and depended on him completely. As he thought about how much he loved her, he realized that she deserved the same respect as he did. It wasn't enough to have a family; you had to be the family. Jack then walked toward Alex and sat down on the steps by the doorway.

"I'm sorry, I didn't get a good enough look at the picture. Let me see it again, sweetie," Jack said, as he patted the space next to him, motioning Alex to sit with him.

It was a beautiful picture of Jack, Eve, and Alex. As Jack studied the picture, he noticed that Alex drew him even larger, in proportion, than he actually was to her. And for the first time in a long while he felt the pride of being larger than life to her, as well as having the responsibility of being the father, and being the family.

Eve then came over to the two of them, and looked at the picture. Sitting there with his wife and daughter, staring at this simple but simply beautiful picture, Jack realized one thing. This was it. This was what life was really about. The show is right here.

As Jack looked at Eve she smiled at him. Then still smiling, she mimed swinging a golf club. Jack stared in surprise and then began to smile in return. He saw a glimmer of the spark that they once shared. It was just for a moment, but that moment was enough to let him know that they could get it all back. Perhaps Eve in her wisdom knew that Jack had to take some personal journey to get back to where they once were. As Jack again looked at Eve, he realized that it was her support that allowed him to take that journey.

Peter once told Jack that it was that one perfect putt or drive that got every golfer addicted to the game. Although perfection is impossible to sustain, he said, by acting as one, completing the circle, finding our unique gift, being the game, and realizing that the show is, indeed, right here, we can create excellence.

Jack knew there was a lot of work ahead of him and Eve to get them to a new special place, but he now understood one thing. They could create the excellence they once shared. And the show really is right here.

The Present

It had been a year since Jack's life-changing meeting with Peter, and life was good. Jack had more confidence than he had ever had in his life. He and Eve were doing better than they had in years. Jack, Eve, and Alex had a renewed sense of their special family. These were all works in progress, but progress was being made. The hospital was busier than ever, due to better customer service, which led to more customer referrals. And their expanded maternity ward led to a new family of customers. These new families would be the future of the hospital. The mood at the hospital was one of positive possibilities, of a team playing to win, and it felt really good.

The last straw was that Neil and Jack actually became friends. After the meeting Neil met with Jack. He explained that he was just so scared of losing his job, and was addicted to an old way of doing things. Jack, in an effort to let him know that he was a strong part of the team, bought Neil a golf lesson with Peter. Neil came back with an ingenious golf and business tip called pull vs. push. The concept was that you let what was unique about a golf hole or a customer, pull you in, as opposed to simply trying to push your way through. Jack realized it was an extension of the U factor, and was thankful for the tip. Neil had learned to flow with the positive current of change. All in all, Jack was a happy man.

Jack was on a golf outing with Ms. Bochard, Maria, who had since been promoted to nurse manager, and Ted. After that meeting, Bochard asked Jack how he had brought down customer complaints. Although Jack felt a little silly at first, he explained about his golf guru and his conversations with Maria. As it turned out Bochard was a big golf enthusiast as well, and was fascinated with the correlations between lessons in golf and business. In fact, it became a little game of theirs to try and discover new connections.

So now every couple of months Jack, Maria, Bochard, and one of the other executives in the hospital would play, seeing if they could uncover some of life's secrets through golf. Jack's friend Ted was subbing for a last-minute cancellation.

"I know your golf guru helped change around our work and your life, but I think you might need a few more lessons, if you want him to help you beat me," Maria said with a small laugh.

"I can't think of anyone else I'd rather lose to, but you may have a point." They both laughed as Jack knew he'd again be buying her lunch the following week.

Bochard overheard them and joined in the laugh, as she had everyone beat by six strokes.

"OK, OK, I need to take another lesson with Peter," joked Ted, who unfortunately was high man on the scoring pole.

As they were walking out, Bochard came up by Jack's side and leaned into him in a half-whisper, "Jack, we discussed it and we'd like you to join our executive committee. I'll go over the details on Monday." Bochard then leaned toward Jack again as they continued walking. "Oh, in case you've ever wondered, it was me who left you that e-mail to 'prepare for change'. It was positive reinforcement. I knew you'd come through."

As Jack drove home, a wonderful feeling came over him. It was as if life finally made sense. All of it. The things we do. The dreams we have. The bonds and relationships we form. It all seemed to fit like a perfect puzzle for Jack.

As he pulled into the driveway, he was looking forward to a nice quiet evening with Eve and Alex. Eve had begun taking a gourmet cooking class and the results were usually quite good. Jack envisioned opening the front door and some new, unique, delectable scent consuming him.

As he opened the door, he couldn't believe what he was hearing. It was Bernie Seethers's "Tin Roof Blues" and that human trombone. Had this all been some crazy dream? Was Bernie Seethers still alive? Was Peter some figment of his imagination? Was Neil still a challenge? Was Bochard still questioning his job? Had his relationship with Eve and Alex not changed? As Jack walked in the door and tried to shake off his confusion, he heard it louder, the "Tin Roof Blues" and the trombone. What was happening? Jack held on tightly to the rail and walked upstairs to where he heard the music, now even louder than before. As he stood outside the door, the music continued to play, along with the human trombone.

Jack took a deep breath, slowly turned the handle of the door, pushed the door open, and got the surprise of his life. Sitting on the floor mouthing the trombone was his daughter Alex and Jenny Heartman from the hospital, while "Tin Roof Blues" played on the CD player.

"Daddy, Daddy, this is my new friend from ballet, Jenny! Look, Daddy, she taught me how to play the trombone to this old music. Listen, Daddy. Listen!"

It turned out that Jenny Heartman had gone into complete remission, which Jack knew about. He just had no idea that she'd return to normal life so quickly.

"Daddy, Daddy, have you ever heard anything like

this?" Alex said beaming with the pride that only an eight-year-old learning something new could have.

"No, not quite like this," Jack said, smiling at his daughter and Jenny.

Jenny smiled at Jack. He wasn't sure if she remembered him or not, but it didn't really matter.

As Jack sat back and watched Alex and Jenny mouthing their trombones it occurred to him again.

The show really is right here!

Implementation Planner

Name:

Organization:

ACT AS ONE

1. What is our team goal?

2. What initiatives will help us achieve that goal?

3. How can departments work together to create seamless service?

COMPLETE THE CIRCLE

1. What procedures can we make predictable?

2. How can we clearly communicate to our customers that we have completed the circle?

3. What standards should we implement?

4. Which customers and staff members do we need to complete the circle?

5. Which people in our life should we complete the circle with?

THE U FACTOR

1. What can we UNCOVER about our customers' needs?

2. What are the UNIQUE UNDULATIONS about a particular client's personality that will help us better UNDERSTAND him/her?

3. How can we best be OURSELF when we interact with him/her?

4. How can our organization/unit turn our uniqueness into a competitive advantage?

THE SHOW'S RIGHT HERE

1. What is most important in my life?

    a.

    b.

    c.

2. What can I do to avoid distractions and stay focused?

3. What can I do to be present in all my interactions?

The Golf Guru

Peter Belmont was featured by ESPN as "Golf's most complete teacher." He won 123 of 124 matches, and holds records at 13 courses. Mr. Belmont is the inventor of the club head variable weighting system used throughout the world and has recently invented the reverse aerodynamic club model.

Peter Belmont is the Proprietor of Belmont Golf Complex located at 824 Ethan Allen Highway (Route 7) in Ridgefield, CT.

ORDER FORM

How to Use this Book:
Buy it for colleagues. Share the powerful lessons that inspired you.
Buy it for your employees. Have every employee read it to enhance employee pride and customer service.
Buy it for your boss. Demonstrate initiative by suggesting this for your organization.
Buy it for your customers. Show your commitment to service by sending a signed copy.
Buy it for business prospects. Build connections and generate new business leads.

How to Order:
For online orders, e-mail request to: www.barbara@golfbusinessonline.com
For telephone orders, call: (203) 894-9400
For secure fax, fax this order form to: (203) 894-9100

> For orders over 2,500 books call for special pricing and ask about customizing the design of the "golf ball" with your company name or logo.

Name: Title:
Company:
Shipping Address:

Phone#:   E-mail:

Prices:
1–4 books_____@ $16.95 = $ _____ S + H $3.00
5-24 books_____@ $15.00 = $ _____S+H $9.00
25-99 books_____@ $12.75 = $ _____S+H $16.00
100-499 books_____@ $11.75 = $ _____S+H $35.00
500-999 books_____@ $10.75= $ _____S+H $55.00
1,000-2,500 books_____@ $ 9.75= $_____S+H $95.00
$_____ Total

Credit Card Information: Circle card used (VISA/MC/Amex)

Name on card_____

Card # _____Exp date_____